Happy 29th Birthday, Sean —
and happy reading!
        Lots of love always,
                Mom

Dale Earnhardt Jr.

The Driving Force

of a New Generation

Beckett Publications Dallas, Texas

Copyright © 2000 by Beckett Publications

All rights reserved under International and
Pan-American Copyright Conventions.

Printed in Canada

Published by:

Beckett Publications

15850 Dallas Parkway

Dallas, Texas 75248

ISBN: 1-887432-86-8

Beckett® is a registered trademark of Beckett
Publications.

First Edition: April 2000

Beckett Corporate Sales and Information

(972) 991-6657

Contributors

Juliet Macur, who interviewed Terry Labonte for
the foreword and Jeff Green for Chapter 5, covers
auto racing for the *Orlando Sentinel* in Orlando,
Florida.

Mike Hembree, who wrote Chapters 1 and 2 and
interviewed Steve Park for Chapter 6, covers auto
racing for the *Greenville News* in Greenville, South
Carolina.

Tom Gillispie, who interviewed Sean Graham for
Chapter 3 and Buddy Baker for Chapter 8, and
wrote Chapter 4, is a freelance writer based in
Kernersville, North Carolina.

Monte Dutton, who interviewed Mark Martin for
Chapter 7, covers auto racing for the *Gaston
Gazette* in Gastonia, North Carolina.

Photography

AP/Wide World Photos: 42, 117, 123

Kathy Bond: 15, 32, 41, 43, 44, 45, 46, 48, 50 (bottom
    left), 52, 53, 54, 55, 56, 58, 59

Jeff Burk: 21 (bottom right)

Chobat Racing Images: 20 (top), 27, 34, 35, 37, 64, 95,
    104, 120, 121

CIA Stock Photography: 51, 100, 125

John Cordes/Sports Imagery: 26

Scott Cunningham: 10, 36, 38, 40 (bottom), 118

Daytona Racing Archives: 39, 40 (top), 68 (top)

Mike Dehoog/TDP: 122 (bottom), 124

Duomo: 25 (right)

Gary Eller/CIA Stock Photography: 74, 81 (bottom),
    111

Jon Ferrey/Allsport: 5

Don Grassman/CIA Stock Photography: 81 (top), 82

Chris Hamilton: 9

Harold Hinson: 18, 20 (bottom), 22, 23 (bottom), 24,
    50 (top), 66 (bottom), 68 (bottom), 78, 80 (top),
    92–93, 94, 99, 105, 106 (top), 107 (top), 112, 119

Craig Jones/Allsport: 76, 110

Allen Kee: 2, 16, 17 (top), 25 (left), 50 (bottom right),
    84

Nigel Kinrade: 1, 8, 17 (bottom), 23 (top), 60, 62, 63,
    65, 66 (top), 67, 71, 85, 90, 91 (bottom), 96–97,
    102, 106 (bottom), 107 (bottom), 108 (bottom),
    109, 116, 122 (top)

Courtesy of Martha Labonte: 12

Ernest Masche/CIA Stock Photography: 80 (bottom)

John Soohoo: 6–7

Brian Spurlock: 21, 30, 79, 88, 91 (top), 108 (top), 114

Jamie Squire/Allsport: 28

David Taylor/Allsport: 77

George Tiedemann/*Sports Illustrated*: 13

contents

Dale Earnhardt Jr.

foreword

BY TERRY LABONTE

As Told to Juliet Macur

Yeah, racing could be in the genes. If you look at families like the Pettys or the Earnhardts, or my brother and me, you can sort of see it.

But I think it's more from growing up around racing than being born with it. I can remember my dad had a shop in his backyard and used to keep the race car back there. I would go out there when I was five or six years old and he'd let me beat the dents out of it with a hammer — or at least try to.

Then, when I was about seven years old, he had some friends that had a quarter midget, and they invited us out to a track to watch them. That's when dad asked me, "Would you like to drive one of those?" I said, "Yeah, but not with all these people here."

So that was it. I got a quarter midget for my birthday or something and we had a big project. We had something to do together

For the Labontes, just like the Earnhardts, racing is a family affair. Terry caught the fever racing quarter midgets at age seven; younger brother Bobby soon followed suit.

in our spare time and every weekend.

My dad had a full-time job working on a Navy base in Corpus Christi, Texas, so he got off work at 3:30 and we would work on cars until nine or ten o'clock at night. Racing was just a hobby we did together. Instead of going fishing or going to the beach or going to the lake, we went racing. But not all families are like that.

It was different with Dale Jr. and his dad, because his dad was so

busy and Dale Jr. didn't live with him. Dale Jr. is from Dale's first marriage, so Dale Jr. was with his mother. When you don't live with your dad and don't spend a lot of time with him, it's hard. It's just different.

With my son Justin, it wasn't that way. He was like my shadow everywhere I went. Whatever I was doing he was right behind me, whether it was fishing or whatever. We were buddies.

I've got a picture of him when he was little sitting in victory lane in Rockingham with a tiny uniform on and his hat cocked to the side. He was all dirty and looked like he had been working on the car all day. That's what probably got him into racing: just being around it and getting interested in it. Now he'll probably run a few races in Busch next year, then maybe go full time the year after that.

I don't think being the son of a Winston Cup champion helps Justin, or any kid, trying to make it in racing. I think people look at them differently and probably expect more from them and think that they've had everything handed to them — and that's really not the case.

You can't just hand someone a race car and expect them to win, because experience is so much a part of it. And you can't get it sitting on top of the toolbox during a race or sitting on top of the truck watching it. You've got get out there and do it yourself. You've got to learn it yourself.

That's how you've got to get interested in racing. You can't just get dragged into it by someone, or be pressured into it because your dad does it. My dad was involved with racing, so I became interested in it, then pursued it. Then Bobby came along, and he grew up around it and wanted to do it. It's just something that's been in our family.

It's not really something that our father wanted us to do or pushed us to do. He didn't really care if we wanted to do it or not. That's the way it is with Justin. I never wanted him to feel like he had to race because I was doing it. I've told him

that so many times he's probably sick of me telling him that. But if he really wants to do it, I'll support him all the way.

I think racing tends to run in the family because a lot of kids do what their parents do or what their dad does. It's like a lot of people who work in the coal mines for generations, or different occupations like fisherman and things like that. If you're brought up around something, you like it.

Dale Jr. was more content following his own pursuits than those of his father's.

Terry fended off Hendrick Motorsports teammate Jeff Gordon, as well as Dale Jarrett and Dale Earnhardt, to capture the 1996 Winston Cup championship.

But then there's the opposite. My dad's parents worked in the paper mill, and he lied about his age so he could get in the Navy. He wanted to leave town early because he didn't want to work in paper mills. So really, either you love to do what your parents do, or you run in the opposite direction.

Dale Jr. kind of did both. He's a driver just like his dad, but he's kind of a free spirit otherwise. Dale Sr. and I started out in Winston Cup the same year, our rookie year, in

1979. We've been hunting a couple times, but Dale Jr. has no interest in what Dale Sr. does. He would never come along. He's just a different kind of guy and wants to do his own thing.

It's hard to be that way when people put so much pressure on you because you're Dale Earnhardt's son. People will look at him and expect him to accomplish the same things in Winston Cup that his dad did. But it'll be different when Dale Jr. moves up to Winston Cup. It's just so much different than Busch. It's not harder; it's just different. People go from Busch to Cup all the time and can't do what they did before.

For one, Dale Sr. has that reputation on the track for running over people. He ran over a lot of people and won a couple of races doing that. He just got away with it, but I don't think Dale Jr. could get away with it if he tried to race like that.

The sport has changed so much. It isn't rednecks in the infield anymore, so you can't just wreck a guy and expect to not hear about it the next day. We've got educated people

Unlike Dale and Dale Jr., Terry and Justin lived in the same household and spent every free moment together — at least until Justin began racing professionally.

now, and we've got corporate sponsors who bring business people to the track. People are going to give you a real hard time about that.

But the newer generation just has to do its own thing. They're going to be good drivers not because their dads were good drivers. They're going to be good because they're talented and they work hard. And Dale Jr.'s got that going for him.

Oh yeah, he's a natural. He's got to have a lot of talent to get in the Busch series and do what he's done. That's impressive. He does a good job. He's got a good team. He'll do a great job just like his dad did, just like his granddad did. He's got a big name to live up to.

Terry Labonte is a two-time winner of the Winston Cup series, claiming points championships in 1984 and 1996. In all "Texas Terry" has amassed twenty-one Winston Cup victories and more than $20 million in prize money.

Labonte says Junior may have a tough time making the leap from Busch to Winston Cup in 2000, but he believes Dale will ultimately be successful. "He's a natural," Labonte says.

what's in a name?

By Mike Hembree

"People want to see if we're going to have a modern version of his dad. But a lot of the attraction is that he's his own individual. He does his own thing." — Steve Crisp, Dale Earnhardt, Inc.

No new driver in NASCAR Winston Cup history has created as much interest as Dale Earnhardt Jr.

In part because of the last name he carries, and in part because of the talent he has exhibited in the Busch Grand National series, Dale Earnhardt Jr. storms into Winston Cup racing in 2000 with high expectations and a fan following already so huge that it dwarfs those of many established Winston Cup racers.

Only twenty-five years old, Earnhardt stands on the brink of what could be one of the most remarkable careers in auto racing. He has a rich sponsorship package provided by Anheuser-Busch, strong team backing from his father's formidable racing operation

Junior whipped fans into a frenzy with his first Busch victory in Texas in 1998, prompting Dale Earnhardt Inc. president Don Hawk to purchase a larger souvenir rig for stock car's new favorite son.

Fans of the Intimidator, of course, are quick to jump on Junior's bandwagon. But Rusty Wallace fans also have taken a liking to Little E. "People who like Rusty will come up and say, 'Junior, I like you because you're a lot like Rusty. You don't take any bull. You don't let anybody push you around,'" says Dale Earnhart Inc.'s Steve Crisp.

and family ties that guarantee him notice wherever he goes and whatever he does.

The promise of his popularity was established in April 1998 when he won the Coca-Cola 300 Busch race at Texas Motor Speedway, the first of what would become a string of wins in the division. After the race, Earnhardt's souvenir trailers at the speedway quickly sold out of every product they carried. T-shirts, caps, model cars, key rings — everything was gone.

A phenomenon had been born. It was as if the legions were waiting on Earnhardt to make his move; when he did, they responded.

Don Hawk, president of Dale Earnhardt Inc. and negotiator for all sponsorship and product proposals that come through the doors of Earnhardt's racing complex, immediately ordered a new, larger souvenir rig for Junior. "People are responding to him, and a lot of that is the name and the mystique," Hawk said. "But a lot of it is that he

Amid a media storm, "The Dominator" unveiled his new No. 8 Winston Cup ride at the Coca-Cola 600 on May 30, 1999. Earnhardt started eighth and finished sixteenth.

After testing the waters with five Winston Cup races in 1999, Earnhardt is ready to race with NASCAR's best fulltime this season.

has performed. When you execute on the track or the playing field, it pays off."

Sales of Dale Earnhardt Jr. T-shirts, caps and die-cast cars shot through the roof, and it quickly became evident that those who had attached themselves to this third-generation driver were along for the ride of their lives. Sponsors soon lined up for the opportunity to join the show, and Anheuser-Busch, through its Budweiser brand, won the bidding with a multi-million-dollar, multi-year deal to carry Junior into Winston Cup racing.

When Earnhardt made his Winston Cup debut in the Coca-Cola 600 at Lowe's Motor Speedway near Charlotte, North Carolina, on May 30, 1999, it seemed as if the whole word was watching. No other rookie in the fifty-year history of Winston Cup racing had been written about so much, photographed so many times, videotaped by so many cameras. The buildup to his first race was so huge that the event itself — he started eighth and finished sixteenth — almost was an anti-climax.

How did this guy become so popular so quickly? Why is his every step shadowed by autograph seekers?

The success of second- and third-generation drivers such as Dale Jarrett and Kyle Petty has raised fans' expectations and put added pressure on Junior to win as well.

The answer rests with a variety of factors. He wins races. He drives aggressively. He isn't afraid to question the order of things. He doesn't back away from challenges.

And that last name. It certainly doesn't hurt. He is his father's son.

"Obviously, he gets some attention because of his dad," said Steve Crisp, a Dale Earnhardt Inc. employee who has the formidable task of arranging and managing Junior's crowded and complicated schedule. "You look at the prece-dents that other second- and third-generation drivers have established. Guys such as Dale Jarrett and Kyle Petty. They've all been successful. Everybody automatically thinks, 'OK, here's the next generation of Earnhardts.' And there's naturally some curiosity there.

"People want to see if we're going to have a modern version of his dad. But a lot of the attraction is that he's his own individual. He does his own thing. A lot of times he may say or do something that's not politically correct. In a way, he's a breath of fresh air. He's a guy who says what's on his mind. If he gets in trouble for it, he'll take the knock over the head for it. To a degree, people like to see that."

Earnhardt has had on-track misadventures with several drivers and has emerged from virtually all encounters with his Chevrolet pointing forward — aggressively so. In the first race of his first full Busch season, he wrecked spectacularly on the Daytona International Speedway backstretch, sending his car into spiraling flight. Only two weeks later, he finished second at Las Vegas, then third at Nashville. By early spring, he was in victory lane for the first time.

"I don't know if his style is like mine," said his father, whose take-no-prisoners approach to racing made him one of motorsports' biggest stars. "He's aggressive at the wheel. He drives the car every lap. That's what we've done in the past. You've got to do it now. It's too competitive not to."

In his first Busch season,

"I don't know if his style is like mine. He's aggressive at the wheel. He drives the car every lap." — Dale Earnhardt

Earnhardt showed his strength at tracks large and small, backing up the Texas victory with wins at Dover, Milwaukee, California, Indianapolis Raceway Park, Richmond and St. Louis. He won three poles, finished in the top five sixteen times and locked up the series championship simply by starting the season finale in Miami.

In a five-race stretch as summer turned to autumn, Earnhardt fin-ished no worse than eighth, handing those chasing him in the point race a stiff challenge. His run to the championship — and a very similar repeat performance in 1999 — drew comparisons to his father, who became an expert at point racing in his march to seven Winston Cup championships.

"As Junior's career has devel-oped, I think he's very similar to his dad in that he'll do whatever he's got to do," Crisp said. "He won't settle for second place. He'll drive the wheels off the car, and if he bends one every now and then, then that's just what happens."

Earnhardt has had to learn how to race at the top levels of NASCAR while also dealing with an unprecedented amount of pressure from sponsors, news media and other racing publics. It has not been an easy road. Someone always wants

famous fathers and sons

With a father as legendary as Dale Earnhardt Sr., and a pretty famous grandfather too, Dale Jr. can only hope to live up to the Earnhardt name. So far in his short career he has done so. If the trend continues and Dale Jr. becomes a NASCAR powerhouse, the Earnhardts will join some elite company as one of the more accomplished families in stock car racing. Here's a breakdown of NASCAR's other top father-son combinations:

The Pettys
Lee Petty was part of NASCAR from the beginning. He raced in the first sanctioned Winston Cup race and one of the first Daytona 500s, setting the stage for a remarkable career that included three Winston Cup championships and fifty-four career victories (seventh on the all-time win list). Meanwhile, Lee's son Richard was destined to outperform his father. His remarkable 1967 campaign, which included twenty-seven victories and a stretch of ten consecutive wins, earned Richard the nickname "The King." True to his moniker, King Richard dominated NASCAR for years. He amassed seven Winston points titles on his way to a record two hundred wins.

The Jarretts
Few drivers in NASCAR history are as respected as Ned Jarrett whose Hall of Fame career included fifty victories and two Winston Cup titles. And since his retirement, Ned has remained a NASCAR household name as a commentator on ESPN broadcasts. From the broadcast booth Ned has been afforded the privilege of watching his son Dale follow in his footsteps. Dale's already solid career heated up in 1999 when he claimed his first Winston Cup championship, making the Jarretts only the second father-son duo to win a season-long points title. The first? The Pettys.

The Bakers
Buck Backer finally peaked seventeen years after his lackluster debut in 1939, winning consecutive Winston Cup titles in 1956 and 1957. By retirement, Buck had compiled forty-six victories. Meanwhile, son Buddy Baker finished his racing career with far fewer wins (nineteen). But what Buddy lacked in victories he made up for in milestones. Buddy became the first driver to top two hundred mph on an enclosed course; he did so at Talladega. Buddy also was the driver who put an end to Richard Petty's streak of ten straight victories in '67.

The Allisons
Bobby Allison began his racing career in a homemade Cheville, a car with which no one, except for perhaps Bobby, thought he could win. By retirement he proved all the critics wrong with eighty-four career victories and fifty-seven poles. Bobby won one Winston Cup title and was runner-up five times. Son Davey Allison also enjoyed a successful career — he was the first driver to win multiple races his rookie season — but that career was cut short by tragedy. In 1993, while challenging for the points championship, Davey was killed in a helicopter accident. He already had won nineteen times in a career full of promise.

a few moments of his time, stealing important minutes from his primary concern: the race car. Before his full-time Winston Cup career even began, he had perfected the art of avoiding reporters so that he could spend more time with his team.

"What you learned last year and the year before that, and even last week, you forget," Earnhardt said. "You go off and do three or four appearances, then you forget everything, and by the time you get in the car again it's like it's the first time. You just feel like you're getting behind.

"It's sort of like you're taking a test and everybody in the whole class except you gets to study."

The presence of those pressures has made Earnhardt's success even more impressive. In the middle of the spotlight, with everybody tugging at him, he has won and won repeatedly, building momentum toward the launch of a full-time Winston Cup career.

When he started the year at Daytona, he found thousands of fans ready to cheer him on. He has inherited many of the devoted followers of his father, and he has made fans of his own. All in all it's a formidable group, one that buys souvenirs in bulk and one that will defend its Earnhardt allegiance to the very end.

"Dale has gotten a lot of his father's fans, but he's also gotten a lot of Rusty Wallace fans," Crisp said. "People who like Rusty will come up and say, 'Junior, I like you because you're a lot like Rusty. You don't take any bull. You don't let anybody push you around.' Then there's a whole new group of fans that follow Junior that maybe didn't pay much attention to racing before. You've got kids in their late teens and early twenties who can relate to Junior. So it's a large segment — old fans, young fans."

Now they, the sponsors, the media — and just about everyone else for that matter — are ready to see Dale make the big move. The world will be watching.

learning the hardt way

By Mike Hembree

"Dad has earned everything he's got with hard work. He's very stern. He knows what you're capable of doing and he expects that every time."
— Dale Earnhardt Jr.

Dale Earnhardt Sr. has won seven Winston Cup championships, dozens of NASCAR races and much more money than he ever could have imagined in his childhood days in the textile mill village of Kannapolis, North Carolina.

Earnhardt, who once lived from payday to payday while trying to establish himself in auto racing, now lives on Easy Street, his decades of success producing a total of more than $33 million in winnings.

When Dale Earnhardt Jr. began showing an interest in racing, his father's financial standing obviously placed him in position to fund almost any endeavor Junior chose to pursue — from racing to rocket science. It didn't work that way.

Earnhardt wanted Junior to learn the sport from the ground up, or, perhaps more accurately, from the garage floor up. He showed him how to get started, then let him find his way.

Earnhardt Sr. had had much the same experience with his dad, Ralph Earnhardt. A NASCAR Late Model Sportsman national champion who built a reputation as one of the best short-track drivers in stock car racing history, Ralph was stacking up race victories during Dale's child-

Junior grew up around the racetrack, so it was only a matter of time before Dale Earnhardt's namesake decided to give the family business a try.

hood, and his son longed to follow in his tire tracks. Dale Sr. was beginning to build his career in 1973 when his father died of a heart attack.

When Dale Jr. decided as a teenager that he'd like to try auto racing, he started much as his grandfather and father had. He didn't have the best cars, the best

engines or the best parts, but he had a desire to learn and advance, and he was willing to spend the night under the belly of a race car, working out the dirty details with used tools.

As Junior started running Street Stock and Late Model Stock races at short tracks in the Carolinas, fans nodded in recognition and assumed that this namesake of one of racing's all-time greats was coming into the sport with his way paved with resources and all the help his famous father could provide. But it wasn't so.

"One of my worst fears is that that perception is going to be there," Earnhardt Jr. said. "I would hate to have people think that. There was no silver spoon — a plastic one, if anything. He wouldn't even give me a job at the shop until I was eighteen.

"I would hate for anybody to perceive this as something that was handed to me. I just look over the past few years at what kind of work

we've put into it to get to where we are. Sometimes I wake up and I feel surprised to be where I am, but then on other days I feel like we've really worked hard to get here and that we deserve it. It's kind of a roller coaster of emotions."

Dale Sr. struggled as a young husband and father to build race cars in his garage and make them winners at short tracks across the region. Working day-time jobs and pouring his free time into car preparation, he built enough of a reputation to place himself in position to move to the Winston Cup Series. He wanted his son to appreciate the sacrifice and work needed to go to the front.

"We built our Late Model Stock cars in the corner of the shop because that's the only room we had," Junior said. "Then you haul it to Myrtle Beach (South Carolina),

Ralph Earnhardt was a NASCAR Late Model Sportsman national champion considered one of the best short-track drivers in stock car racing history before dying young from a heart attack.

and you've got to go down there and win to show that you can do it. Then, when you do, there's no better feeling than that. It's sort of like the old days.

"Dad has earned everything he's got with hard work. He's very stern. He knows what you're capable of doing and he expects that every time."

Before he became a full-time race car driver, Junior had a job pumping gas. He later worked for two years changing oil in the service department of his father's Newton, North Carolina, Chevrolet dealership. "Then one day I decided to leave and try driving race cars," he said.

Junior raced in the Street Stock division at Concord Motor Speedway near Charlotte, then moved up to Late Model Stock, benefiting from the knowledge and assistance of veteran mechanic Gary Hargett of Marshville, North Carolina. Then Earnhardt Sr. gave Junior the use of a corner of his race shop and left car preparation to Junior and young mechanic Wesley Sherrill.

"That was the way we planned for it to happen," Junior said. "I wanted to work on the cars on my own so I could learn everything about it. It was mostly me and Wesley. He and I were about equally competent working on cars. I learned a lot just by doing it, by being around it, and just by having

Dale Jr. and Wes Sherrill were allowed use of a corner of Senior's race shop where the two learned how to build a winning race car. "A lot of what we did was hit and miss," Sherrill says.

a little common sense. A lot of it was trial and error.

"I really didn't learn enough. I wish I'd paid more attention than I did and studied a little harder because there's still things I need to learn."

Sherrill, now a mechanic at Dale Earnhardt, Inc., said Dale Sr. "put

us in the ball game and said, 'Here it is. Learn to work on it and make it roll.' We worked in the old Deerhead Shop (so-called because it is decorated with hunting trophies Dale Sr. has claimed through the years). We were there from 8 a.m. until sometimes ten or eleven at night, depending on what happened the week before.

"A lot of what we did was hit and miss. Dale Jr. had some decent notes from his time with Gary Hargett, and his memory is good. And we talked with a lot of people who had been at the tracks we went to. Dale has a real good feel for cars. He knows what he wants."

Randy Earnhardt, Dale Jr.'s uncle, managed the Late Model racing efforts of Junior, his brother Kerry and his sister Kelley. Now director of purchasing and inventory control at Dale Earnhardt, Inc., Randy said Junior quickly showed an appreciation for the finer points of racing.

"That's all he ever focused on," he said. "All he cared about was driving that car. I took him to a trade

Junior's mom, Brenda Jackson, has supported her son's endeavors as best she can. But work commitments have kept Brenda, who divorced Dale when Junior was two, from attending all of Junior's races.

show once, and he went around and visited every carburetor manufacturer that was there and wound up getting carburetors from all of them. He used to keep them under his bed at night because he was afraid one of the other kids would get them. He'd hide them under the bed."

With Earnhardt and Sherrill turning wrenches, they made enough progress in Late Models to move toward the next step: Busch Grand National racing. Earnhardt made his series debut at Myrtle Beach Speedway in 1996, then ran eight BGN races in 1997 — six in Earnhardt family cars and two in cars owned by Ed Whitaker. The

Junior honed his skills at Myrtle Beach beginning in 1994, racing Late Model Stock before graduating to the Busch series. "I think the years he raced his own Late Model are the years when he learned the most," says Tony Eury Sr., Earnhardt's Busch Grand National crew chief.

1998 season marked his first full-time run in Busch cars, and he quickly cashed in on his promise, winning seven races and the national championship.

The years Earnhardt spent fine-tuning his own cars in short-track racing quickly paid dividends as he raced to wins on one of motorsports' most competitive circuits.

"He's real mechanical, and I think that comes from being a student of the sport," Steve Hmiel said of Earnhardt. As technical director for Dale Earnhardt, Inc., Hmiel has oversight over all car-building decisions in the Earnhardt operation.

"He has an understanding of what's going on," Hmiel said. "He's a lot like his daddy in that. He knows about things that are happening around him, and he uses that knowledge to his advantage."

The beating and banging of the Late Model Stock years, and nights spent in the shop repairing damage from accidents and mistakes, gave Earnhardt a solid foundation to succeed quickly at the higher levels.

"I think the years he raced his own Late Model are the years when he learned the most," said Tony Eury Sr., Earnhardt's BGN crew chief. "His daddy made him do his own work. He was doing his own adjusting at the race track, and you learn a lot that way. When they started going to different tracks, that helped him a lot. You have to make changes, and you can only learn by doing it.

Dale made his Busch series debut in 1996 at Myrtle Beach, finishing fourteenth in the Carolina Pride/Advance Auto 250.

"(In 1998) he got better all year long at coming in and telling us what the car needed. That's kind of why we got better as the year went along. We started hitting on stuff, and he knew what it was going to do when we changed something. The more he's learned, he can come in and say that the rear springs are too stiff or the right front springs are too soft or whatever. He's kept moving toward that point, and that's what makes a good driver.

"As tough as this sport is today and with no more practice than you get when you get to the track, you have to be ready. Somebody that doesn't know race cars and has never worked on race cars isn't going to make it in this business. There's just not enough time at the race track to make things right, and the fields are so close that if you're off a little — you're off a lot."

Earnhardt raced in five Winston Cup events in 1999 as a prelude to his greatly anticipated graduation to full-time Cup racing in 2000. The handful of races, along with frequent interaction with Winston Cup drivers in the Busch series, gave him a chance to get on solid footing in a series that presents a rude awakening to newcomers.

"Hopefully, some of those guys will be more comfortable racing with me knowing that I have a little common sense about it," Earnhardt said. "That's the biggest part. What's most important to them is that you're smart as a race car driver. They don't want you out there making a lot of mistakes, and they don't want you to be difficult to be around on the race track."

Thanks to Dale Sr. and his hands-off approach, Junior should be ready.

dale jr. timeline

Oct. 10, 1974	Ralph Dale Earnhardt Jr. is born in Concord, North Carolina
1992	At age seventeen Dale Jr. begins his professional racing career by competing in the Street Stock Division at Concord Speedway.
1994	With two seasons of experience, Earnhardt begins racing in the NASCAR Late Model Stock Division.
June 22, 1996	Dale Jr. finishes fourteenth in his first Busch Grand National Start in the Carolina Pride/Advance Auto 250 at Myrtle Beach.
March 28, 1998	Dale begins a Busch race as the pole-setter for the first time in the Moore's Snacks 250 at Bristol.
April 4, 1998	In the Coca-Cola 300 race at Texas Motor Speedway, "Little E" earns his first career Busch series victory.
Sept. 21, 1998	Budweiser announces a sponsorship deal involving Earnhardt Jr. on the Winston Cup circuit. The partnership is set to last through the 2004 season.
Nov. 14, 1998	After the last race of the season, Dale becomes the official 1998 BGN champion. It is the first time a third generation racer has won a NASCAR championship.
May 30, 1999	Dale Jr. races to a sixteenth-place finish in his first Winston Cup start, the Coca-Cola 600 at Lowes Motor Speedway.
Nov. 7, 1999	Earnhardt Jr. follows up his 1998 Busch success by clinching a second consecutive championship at Phoenix International Raceway.

short track to success

BY SEAN GRAHAM
As Told To Tom Gillispie

> "I guess he was held to a higher standard than somebody off the street. When your dad's in Winston Cup and a star — Dale Earnhardt, of all people — folks expect you to drive like your dad."
> — Sean Graham

A whole bunch of us raced against Dale Jr. A lot of Winston Cup sons go to Myrtle Beach to race. Adam Petty was there. Several others were there, too.

I raced against Dale in 1997. He was a good racer. He started out with us in Late Model Stock. Dale was learning and maturing, but he was a good, clean racer.

Sometimes he acted kind of hesitant with us, sometimes he'd go off to himself, but he got to know everybody. He was one of us. The thing of it was, I knew he'd be there the whole season. He was learning, so he had to stay to learn.

I got to know him pretty good. In fact, this year, I saw him at Myrtle Beach at the Busch race. I said, "Hey," and we talked a minute.

"When he started out with us, he wasn't very aggressive," Graham says. "Then he started taking more chances. He'd go under a car where there was no room on the racetrack, and he went under there anyway. And then some room opened up and he was there . . ."

Dale Jr. is one of many sons of famous stock car drivers to begin their racing careers on the short tracks in the Carolinas. Other regulars at Myrtle Beach included Adam Petty (above) and Justin Labonte (left).

Junior's brother Kerry and sister Kelly have raced on the short track circuit as well. Kerry even went head-to-head with Junior in the Busch series in 1999, competing in four races for the Channellock team.

When he raced us at Myrtle Beach, he had the best people with him, and that helped, of course. You can't do it without people and equipment, and he had that.

I think that, yeah, people probably raced him a little harder than someone not named Earnhardt, although it shouldn't matter. When we were racing together, I might have raced him a little harder because he was an Earnhardt, too. But he was just like any other racer; he was trying to win the race.

I guess he was held to a higher standard than somebody off the street. When your dad's in Winston Cup and a star — Dale Earnhardt, of all people — folks expect you to drive like your dad. I guess he didn't

Above: Adam Petty in the No. 49 NWO car.
Below: Dale found the wall in his No. 3 late model stock car every now and then, but fellow racer Graham says Junior never suffered a major collision.

drive like his dad, but he was a good driver.

The thing was, he *was* different. He was in a different situation than we were. We just assumed he was going somewhere no matter what he did in Late Model Stock, just because of who he is. They put him in Late Model Stock to get him some experience. It was the same thing when Adam Petty ran with us.

Jamie Skinner, Mike Skinner's son, and Terry Labonte's son, Justin, have run Late Model for experience, too.

I always ran well at Myrtle Beach, and we'd talk about how to get around the track, what springs I was using. At the drivers' meeting, we'd sit around and start talking. I started talking to him, and he'd ask, "How do you get around here so well?" Sometimes the guy working on his car (Wesley Sherrill) talked to me, asked me the same thing.

Dale acted the same all the time with us. He was quiet, and he never walked around like a big shot.

When he started out with us, he wasn't very aggressive. Then he

"Dale acted the same all the time with us," Graham says. "He was quiet, and he never walked around like a big shot."

Earnhardt's
confidence
grew with
each race,
and it showed
on the track
where Junior
would make
some daring
moves to
work his way
through the
pack.

started taking more chances. He'd go under a car where there was no room on the racetrack, and he went under there anyway. And then some room opened up and he was there, and everything was fine.

He was learning when he raced with us, but he never got into bad accidents. I don't think he had a bad wreck as far as tearing up equipment. He was just getting better and better as a driver, getting more aggressive, taking more chances, get-

ting used to it. He wasn't all over the place as a driver. He wasn't a guy who'd get crazy. He drove with some common sense.

Dale Jr. probably learned a lot from us, but the only thing I could learn from him would be what I could learn now. In Late Model Stock, it was the first time he drove, really. There was nothing I could learn from him in Late Model Stock.

If I had the chance to talk to him now, I'd like to ask him about

Busch. I'd like to ask him what it's like to make the transformation from Late Model Stock to Busch.

We run bias-ply tires, Hoosiers, and they run Goodyear radials. They say the hardest thing is to go from bias-ply to radials, because when you go into the corner with bias-plys, you can get into the gas more. You can't do that with radials, I hear. You'll lose it.

The other thing, of course, is that they have a lot more horse-power than we've got. I'd like to talk to him about that.

Junior was a good driver when he raced with us. It's that simple. He was right there with us — a top-five race car every week. In fact, I think he won one race at Myrtle Beach.

I remember one particular scrape

Rising Sons

The short track at Myrtle Beach served as the top training ground for Dale Earnhardt Jr. Week after week Junior honed the talent that eventually would lead him to two Busch series titles in 1998 and 1999. But Dale Jr. is not the only famous son to jumpstart his racing career at Myrtle Beach. The Labontes, Skinners and Pettys have all seen the next generation of racing begin on the track. Here is a look at the respective racing careers of fellow famous sons Adam Petty, Justin Labonte and Jamie Skinner since learning the ropes at Myrtle Beach:

Adam Petty
Two weeks before Adam Petty turned eighteen, he won the Kansas City Excitement 300 at the I-70 Speedway. With the victory he replaced Mark Martin as the youngest driver ever to win an American Speed Association race. The ASA record created a lot of excitement around the Petty household. However, in his first full season of BGN racing in 1999, Adam averaged a starting position of twenty-fourth while averaging a twenty-sixth-place finish in his twenty-nine starts. Petty's best finish was fourth in the Auto Club 300.

Justin Labonte
In 1997, Justin Labonte reigned as the champion of his mini-stock racing division at the Ace Speedway in Burlington, North Carolina. In 1998, he placed third overall in the USAR Hooters ProCup Series. However, this success did not carry over into Justin's 1999 Busch series campaign. In nine starts Labonte's average finish was thirtieth. He also failed to finish three of his nine races. But Terry's son, fresh out of high school, has time on his side and will likely continue to gain experience on the Busch circuit for the next few seasons.

Jamie Skinner
Jamie Skinner has found success in his sixty-four Late Model Stock races since 1996, especially in 1998 when he placed in the top ten in thirteen of eighteen races. He has also qualified in the top ten for two NASCAR Truck series events. The Busch series, though, has proven more difficult to tame for Skinner. In three races he failed to finish better than twenty-ninth, and he finished a dismal forty-third after an accident in his final BGN start in 1999.

between him and me. Our cars hit together, and I hit the wall. It was one of those racing deals, just racing close together. I wasn't mad . . . well, I might have got upset a little, since it tore up my race car. But that happens in the division we're in.

It's good to see the success he's had in Busch Grand National. I'm glad he's doing good. He started off good in Busch, and I think racing at a lot of different short tracks helped. He was better off starting where he did, at places like Concord and Myrtle Beach, than jumping right into a Busch car.

The thing is, though, that I didn't know he was going to jump into Busch Grand National that fast, be that good that fast. It surprised me that he jumped in and — bam! — was that good.

I'm happy for him. He's been a Busch Grand National champion, and I expect he'll be Winston Cup champion, too.

Sean Graham, of Summerville, South Carolina, is a veteran of the Late Model Stock division at Myrtle Beach. Although Graham has been racing for thirteen years, he realizes he may never make the move to the Busch circuit, much less Winston Cup.

"If my dad was Earnhardt, I'd be up there in Busch Grand National, too," Graham says. "Everybody knew that was the way it would be (with Dale Jr. and the other sons of famous drivers at Myrtle Beach)."

But Graham doesn't appear to mind, taking pride in knowing he's made a difference in the development of other future Busch and Winston Cup drivers.

Graham has yet to make the move to the Busch Grand National level, but the Myrtle Beach veteran has done his part to help make Junior reach his goals.

Busch
breakthrough

By Tom Gillispie

"We saw flashes, but I didn't see enough flashes to think '1998 Busch Grand National champion, seven wins, three poles' and all those other accolades."
— Don Hawk

Dale Earnhardt Jr. didn't finish the 1998 Busch Grand National season the way he might have dreamed. Oh, he won his first series title, all right, but there was no big bang at the end — unless you count the engine Dale blew in the season-finale Jiffy Lube Miami 300.

Earnhardt Jr. became the '98 Busch champion while sitting in the Homestead, Florida, track's garage after a forty-second place finish, good for next to last.

Junior didn't have to worry, though, since his second-place showing a week earlier at Atlanta gave him a 166-point lead over Matt Kenseth and guaranteed that all he had to do was start the race. So it wasn't great, but it was effective.

Earnhardt captured the pole at Bristol on March 28, but the young driver's first Busch victory would have to wait another week.

Friendly archrival Kenseth finished fourth at Homestead, but Earnhardt Jr. edged Kenseth by forty-eight points (4,469 to 4,421) to capture the series title in his first full season.

"I'm not taking anything away from Matt Kenseth and his bunch," Earnhardt Jr. said of the team led by owner/crew chief Robbie Reiser following the season. "They've done a great job this year. He ran every step of the way there with us, but I think we just had a little bit more luck on our side."

Junior's namesake father, the infamous seven-time Winston Cup champion, had finished his season a week earlier in Atlanta, so he shared victory lane with the newly-crowned champion and everyone made a victory lap or two around the 1.5-mile oval.

It was a season worth celebrating: three poles, a series-high seven victories and a series-high $1,332,701 in earnings (compared to Kenseth's $991,965). Junior even managed to draw NASCAR's wrath, earning a five thousand dollar fine and a ninety-day probation for a bumping incident with Tony Stewart at Pikes Peak.

Still, it was a breakout year for a young driver (twenty-four on October 10, 1998) who, up to that time, had posted twelve poles, three wins, fifty-nine top-five finishes and ninety top-ten finishes in one hundred and thirteen Late Model Stock races. Earnhardt Jr. had run just nine Busch races entering 1998, with his best finish a seventh at Brooklyn, Michigan, in 1997.

It probably helped that Junior was finally able to spend more time with Dale Earnhardt, the owner of his race team. In fact, he got to race

Dad and various other Winston Cup drivers in the postseason exhibition race in Japan. Mostly, Junior listened and absorbed what his dad knows.

"He's a seven-time champion and he's my daddy, but he is also the car owner," Junior said in 1998. "He has the right to get on the radio. Who knows better than him? We pay close attention to what he says and it pays off.

"Sometimes, you get frustrated because the father-son relationship blends in there. But you have to

After this pit stop mishap at the '98 season opener at Daytona, Dale wrecked and finished thirty-seventh.

ACDelco
BUSCH
WINNER
Coca - Cola 300
TEXAS MOTOR SPEEDWAY
APRIL 4, 1998

think about what he has been through, what he knows and how knowledgeable he is."

Junior also earned the respect and friendship of his peers and elders during his remarkable 1998 run, especially Winston Cup veteran Todd Bodine.

"He's not getting a big head. He's keeping his head on his shoulders, and he knows where he's coming from," says Bodine, who has raced both Busch Grand National and Winston Cup the past several years. "He's worked on these cars,

he's helped build them, and he understands how hard it is and how hard those guys work.

"I'm almost as proud of him as his father is. I've always talked with him and had a good relationship, he's a great kid and I'm really happy for him."

Dale Jr. also earned the respect of Kenseth during his first year on the Busch circuit. The two even became good friends.

"It's a lot of fun, really," Earnhardt says of racing against Kenseth. "I've gotten to know him

Opposite: Junior broke through with his first win in April 1998, capturing the checkered flag at the Coca-Cola 300 in Texas. Many more Busch victories would follow.

Below: Earnhardt won a series-high seven races, including the MBNA Platinum 200 at Dover.

Above: Dale appeared to pose little threat to Randy LaJoie at Talladega, finishing thirty-second. But thanks to a midseason winning streak, Earnhardt spoiled LaJoie's bid for a third consecutive Busch series title.
Below: Junior's second-place finish at Atlanta gave him a comfortable 166-point cushion over his buddy Matt Kenseth and allowed him to claim the title by simply starting the following week in Miami.

"We've raced each other hard, whether it was for first or eighth. I hope to keep the competition up. Hopefully, we'll run hard with him for years to come." — Matt Kenseth

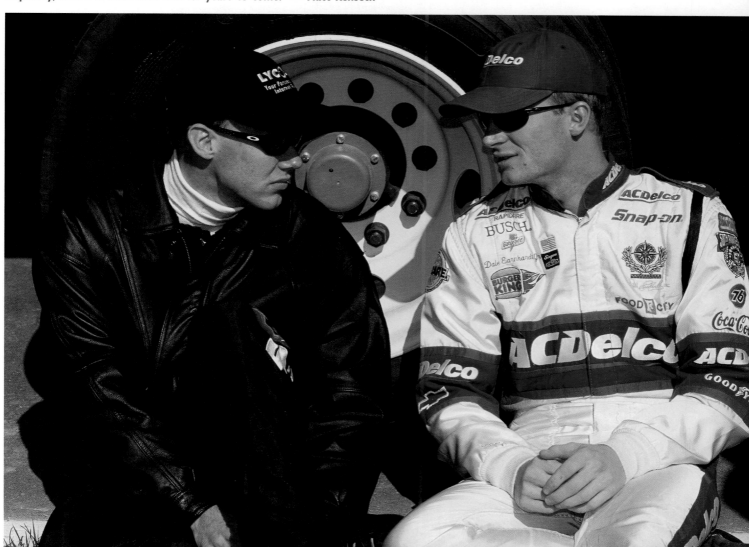

Above: Dale Jr. and family accepted the Busch series championship in style at the Busch Grand National year-end awards banquet. "It's a great team effort, but I'm surely proud of that boy of mine," Dale Sr. told The Associated Press.

Below: When The Dominator was done, he had collected $1,332,701 in earnings — not bad for a driver criticized by many as not yet ready for the big time.

and hang out with him on the weekends. We go out and shoot the crap. I've gotten to know him personally and he's fun to race with. He does so much with so much less. We're pretty good pals. There's always going to be competitiveness. If we can't win it, I'm pulling for him to win it.

"Racing each other on the track is fun because he always races me clean and I always race him clean. We respect each other a lot as far as our racing abilities go, and we don't try anything dirty on the track when we're racing together. That's what it's all about."

Kenseth acknowledges that the rivalry is often intense. During the 1999 Busch campaign, Junior edged Jeff Green and Kenseth, again, for the Busch points title. But that hasn't stopped Kenseth from developing a strong bond with Earnhardt.

"It's a rivalry but a friendly one," says Kenseth, who had produced just two top-five finishes in twenty-two races heading into 1998. "We get along good. He's four years

younger than me, so he makes me feel old. He's been a little better as of late, but racing him has been a lot of fun, knock on wood.

"We've raced each other hard, whether it was for first or eighth. I hope to keep the competition up. Hopefully, we'll run hard with him for years to come."

Certainly, Kenseth and Earnhardt Jr. raced each other hard in 1998. While Kenseth would have his own breakout season with three wins and seventeen top-five finishes (one more than Earnhardt Jr.), "Little E" won a series-high seven races. Junior captured the checkered flag at Texas (Coca-Cola 300), Dover (MBNA Platinum 200), Milwaukee (DieHard 250), California (Kenwood Home & Car Audio 300), Indianapolis (Kroger NASCAR 200), Richmond, Va. (Autolite Platinum 250) and Gateway (Carquest Auto Parts).

But for a while in '98, Dale Jr. looked little like a champion. He had flashes, of course, but something bad always seemed to follow the good.

He started third in the season opener at Daytona, but he wrecked and finished thirty-seventh. After a sixteenth-place finish at Rockingham, Earnhardt Jr. put together a mini-run, finishing second, third, tenth, second, first (Texas) and eighth in successive weeks. But then he placed thirty-second at Talladega, tenth at New Hampshire, twenty-eighth at Nazareth and thirtieth at Charlotte.

Finally, Junior and his crew began hitting on all cylinders. Earnhardt won at Dover, placed second at Richmond and finished eighth on the road course at Watkins Glen. He then kept the streak going with a win at Milwaukee, followed by fifth- and first-place showings, respectively at Myrtle Beach and California.

All of a sudden Earnhardt Jr. had won four races in a nine-race stretch, and it would have been five if he hadn't made a mental mistake while leading at South Boston. While trying to pass the lapped car of Joe Bessey, Junior got a little aggressive, and Bessey spun out.

NASCAR black-flagged the points leader, who went back out later and finished thirteenth.

Junior won the next week at Indianapolis Raceway Park and posted two more victories and a pair of runner-up finishes the rest of the way.

It was a shockingly effective season for the first-year driver. In fact, Dale Earnhardt Inc. president Don Hawk admitted after the season that he and his staff had no idea that Junior would be so good. Not a glimmer.

"We saw flashes, but I didn't see enough flashes to think '1998 Busch Grand National champion, seven wins, three poles' and all those other accolades," Hawk said. "I went to Myrtle Beach, stood on a trailer, and thought, 'This is unique. This is different.' But he exceeded our expectation level and his."

Hawk, who put the youngster in a Budweiser-sponsored Winston Cup car for five races in 1999, said Dale Jr. drove at the level of the competition during his Street Stock and Late Model Stock days at

Concord Motorsport Park and Myrtle Beach Speedway. In other words, he was good but not great.

"He finished third in points, he finished second in points, he won a race or two, he was OK," Hawk said. "But when he moved to the next level, the Busch Series, he just drove at their level. He didn't know anything else. We put him in a Busch car, sent him to a couple of tracks and, guess what, he was fast, he was good."

Actually, he was better than good. He was a champion.

Junior from 1996 to 1998

Busch Grand National Circuit

1996

Date	Event	Track	Type	Make	Finish	Start	Laps	Laps Completed	Status	Earnings
6/22/96	Carolina Pride/Adv. Auto 250	Myrtle Beach	ST	Chevrolet	14	7	250	249	Running	$1,880

Starts	Poles	Wins	Top 5s	Top 10s	DNFs	Laps Raced	Total Earned
1	0	0	0	0	0	249	$1,880

1997

Date	Event	Track	Type	Make	Finish	Start	Laps	Laps Completed	Status	Earnings
4/12/97	Bellsouth Mobility/Opryland 320	Nashville	SS	Chevrolet	39	19	320	93	Mechanical	$2,525
6/29/97	Lysol 200	Watkins Glenn	RC	Chevrolet	39	9	82	12	Engine	$2,725
7/26/97	Inaugural Gateway 300	Gateway International	SS	Chevrolet	38	18	240	61	Accident	$11,400
8/16/97	Detroit Gasket 200	Michigan	SS	Chevrolet	7	18	100	100	Running	$6,295
8/22/97	Food City 250	Bristol	ST	Chevrolet	22	2	250	247	Running	$4,355
10/19/97	Kenwood Home & Car Audio 300	California	SS	Chevrolet	34	11	150	129	Handling	$11,150
10/25/97	AC Delco 200	North Carolina	SS	Chevrolet	16	24	197	197	Running	$4,175
11/9/97	Jiffy Lube Miami 300	Metro Dade-Homestead	SS	Chevrolet	13	14	200	199	Running	$10,315

Starts	Poles	Wins	Top 5s	Top 10s	DNFs	Laps Raced	Total Earned
8	0	0	0	1	4	1,038	$52,880

1998

Date	Event	Track	Type	Make	Finish	Start	Laps	Laps Completed	Status	Earnings
2/14/98	NAPA Auto Parts 300	Daytona	SS	Chevrolet	37	3	120	81	Accident	$21,425
2/21/98	GM Goodwrench Service Plus 200	Rockingham	SS	Chevrolet	16	6	197	197	Running	$12,100
2/28/98	Las Vegas 300	Las Vegas	SS	Chevrolet	2	8	200	200	Running	$59,000
3/15/98	Bell South Mobility/Opryland 320	Nashville	ST	Chevrolet	3	7	320	320	Running	$24,775
3/21/98	Diamond Hill Plywood 200	Darlington	SS	Chevrolet	10	37	147	147	Running	$14,425
3/28/98	Moore's Snacks 250	Bristol	ST	Chevrolet	2	1	250	250	Running	$21,260
4/4/98	Coca-Cola 300	Texas	SS	Chevrolet	1	16	200	200	Running	$66,075
4/11/98	Galaxy Foods 300	Hickory	ST	Chevrolet	8	16	300	300	Running	$13,045
4/25/98	Touchstone Energy 300	Talladega	SS	Chevrolet	32	4	113	43	Handling	$14,300
5/9/98	Gumout Long Life Formula 200	New Hampshire	SS	Chevrolet	10	16	200	200	Running	$13,475
5/17/98	First Union 200	Nazareth	SS	Chevrolet	28	1	188	200	Running	$12,975
5/23/98	Car Quest Auto Parts 300	Charlotte	SS	Chevrolet	30	23	200	175	Running	$13,245
5/30/98	MBNA Platinum 200	Dover	SS	Chevrolet	1	16	200	200	Running	$34,075
6/5/98	Hardee's 250	Richmond	ST	Chevrolet	2	3	250	250	Running	$27,095
6/14/98	Lycos.com 250	Pikes Peak	SS	Chevrolet	10	5	250	250	Running	$24,000
6/28/98	Lysol 200	Watkins Glenn	RC	Chevrolet	8	12	82	82	Running	$14,150
7/5/98	DieHard 250	Milwaukee	SS	Chevrolet	1	2	250	250	Running	$39,625
7/11/98	Myrtle Beach 250	Myrtle Beach	ST	Chevrolet	5	3	250	250	Running	$17,075
7/19/98	Kenwood Home & Car Audio 300	California	SS	Chevrolet	1	2	150	150	Running	$68,175
7/25/98	Lycos.com 300	South Boston	ST	Chevrolet	13	1	300	299	Running	$16,925
7/31/98	Kroger 200	Indy Raceway Park	ST	Chevrolet	1	16	200	200	Running	$34,225
8/15/98	Pepsi 200	Michigan	SS	Chevrolet	5	10	100	100	Running	$19,275
8/21/98	Food City 250	Bristol	ST	Chevrolet	15	4	250	246	Running	$14,490
9/5/98	Dura-Lube 200	Darlington	SS	Chevrolet	2	34	147	147	Running	$28,375
9/11/98	Autolite Platinum 250	Richmond	SS	Chevrolet	1	2	250	250	Running	$35,600
9/19/98	MBNA Gold 200	Dover	SS	Chevrolet	8	17	200	199	Running	$16,590
10/3/98	All Pro Bumper to Bumper 300	Charlotte	SS	Chevrolet	3	5	200	200	Running	$39,325
10/17/98	CarQuest Auto Parts 250	Gateway	SS	Chevrolet	1	13	200	200	Running	$48,525
10/31/98	AC Delco 200	North Carolina	SS	Chevrolet	14	8	197	197	Running	$15,095
11/7/98	Stihl Power Tools 300	Atlanta	SS	Chevrolet	2	6	195	195	Running	$37,925
11/14/98	Jiffy Lube Miami 300	Metro-Dade	SS	Chevrolet	42	15	200	89	Engine	$17,470

Starts	Poles	Wins	Top 5s	Top 10s	DNFs	Laps Raced	Total Earned
31	3	7	16	22	3	6,000	$1,332,701

Sources: *The NASCAR Busch Series Grand National Division Media Guide* and *NASCAR Preview and Press Guide*

the real deal

BY JEFF GREEN
As Told to Juliet Macur

"He's just a natural. Just as soon as he set foot in that No. 3 car, he set the world on fire."
— Jeff Green

South Boston in 1999: That was the first time we really raced as hard as we could race against each other. There's been a few times since then, but South Boston, Virginia, that was the place.

It's just a little bullring of a racetrack (.4-mile oval), and it's not one of the big spotlight Busch races. But that's the thing — it doesn't matter.

We both wanted to win, and we raced with our tongues hanging out. It fit both of our driving styles, so that's what made it fun. It was coming down over the last few laps, and I was right there, right behind him. I could've knocked him out of the way and won the race, I was that close. But I knew he wouldn't have done me that way. It would've come back around.

Dale waged a classic battle with Jeff Green at South Boston, holding off Green down the stretch then celebrating with a mosh-pit style leap into his crew's arms.

And it probably has. He's probably not spun me out, just because he knows I race him clean, too.

I think that I can go to Dale Jr. and get a straight answer and he can come to me and get a straight answer, too. That's one thing he has going for him. His dad won't ever lie to him. I worked for his dad, driving that same car Dale Jr. drove, in 1995 and '96. It was an experience. Every day was an experience.

But with me working there, that's how we got to be as good buddies as we are. I was driving the Busch car, and Dale was still working on and driving Late Models at the time, just gaining experience and getting ready for his future. And he came to me quite a bit. His dad, of course, helped him. But you can go to one of your best buddies and probably ask him something you couldn't go to your dad and ask.

I guess that's why he felt comfortable with me. I felt fortunate to be in that situation, to see him when he wasn't a big deal. He was down there, trying to get up here

(to Busch). I've seen his career pretty much blossom.

But it wasn't pretty at the start. I worked in the Busch shop in those days, and he had his hands full with that Late Model deal. He would go race, tear 'em up, fix 'em up and race 'em again.

It hasn't been an easy road for Dale Jr., and I saw it. He's got to live up to high expectations, and I think he's done a great job. "You're Dale Earnhardt Sr.'s boy — so you better be winning races."

He didn't have that much success racing Late Models, either.

Green forged a strong bond with Junior while driving a Dale Earnhardt Inc. Busch car in 1995 and 1996. "It hasn't been an easy road for Dale Jr., and I saw it." Green says. "He's got to live up to high expectations . . . "

Certainly not as much as he wanted. But I remember him getting that experience of hauling the cars there, and making the cars as good as he could make it. He was doing everything. He didn't have all the tools and people he has now.

That's the way a lot of us grew up. We built our cars out of steel racks and turned them into race cars. That's why Dale Sr. didn't want to just hand Dale Jr. the best stuff.

Dale Sr. didn't give him anything. He made him earn it. He could've gone out and bought the best race cars money could buy. But nah. He made Dale Jr. build 'em and haul 'em to the racetrack, race 'em and haul 'em back, and clean 'em up and fix 'em.

Whatever. I'm sure Senior did

Opposite: When it comes to building a competitive race car, Jeff says Dale listens to as many different viewpoints as possible, then makes his own informed decisions.

Below: Dale fended off NASCAR's brightest star, Jeff Gordon, in the NAPA 200 on Aug. 21, putting himself in position to make a run at another points championship.

Above: Junior captured one of his four poles at Myrtle Beach, but 1999 runner-up Green took the checkered flag.

Right: Dale drove through wrecks and dodged in an out of traffic in a race reminiscent of his Street Stock days to hunt down Mark Martin for the Autolite Platinum 250 trophy, his sixth win in 1999.

Phoenix became the site of an Earnhardt Jr. love-in on November 6 when Dale clinched his second consecutive Busch series title with a second-place finish. Dale Sr. joined the festivities, which included a traditional complete-crew victory lap and the spraying of plenty of Busch beer into an approving crowd.

that on purpose. But undoubtedly, that was the best move ever.

Even when we were working in the same shop, we didn't talk a lot about driving styles, because everybody has a different style. We talked a lot about chassis setup, and he really wanted to learn. He wanted to know what this left-rear spring does, what that right-rear spring does. And he wanted to know, from whoever he could find out from, about building race cars.

He knew everybody's got a different idea about building race cars. Which way's the best way? Who knows? But Junior knew that everybody had different ideas, and I think he took a lot of people's ideas. Hopefully, he took some of mine. And hopefully, that's helped him through his career so far.

He was very eager. I really look up to him in that aspect. Every minute, when he needed to be, he was so attentive and was trying to figure things out. There's no telling where he could've been off to, doing anything. Maybe he could've made it to this point had he been messin'

around, but I don't know. All I know is he was very focused and eager to get there. And he's still got that eagerness.

He's just like his dad. He wants to win every lap. I remember one time, when he was running Late Models, he went to Nashville for a big race, and he wanted me to come with him. I've got a lot of laps around that place, so it made sense.

I went, and I think we both matured that night. We became better friends, and we both learned a lot about racing and race cars from each other. He wanted to win that race, and I wanted the team to win that race. We didn't win it, but we bonded.

Any time you go to a racetrack,

you're going to learn something, and we both realized that. We both learned a lot about each other.

I like Junior's driving style. He'll drive the wheels off of it, no doubt about it. But he knows his limitations. You've got your great drivers, but some great drivers don't know their limitations. I feel like he's going to go a long way because of that.

He knows when to race; he knows when not to race. If you're faster, he's going to let you go. When he gives you a position, he knows in the back of his mind that you're better at that point.

Now, he's thinking, and he knows that twenty laps later in the race, it might be a different situation. He'll just race you later, because he's learned that these races are too long to fight over nothing. That's a big part of our game: race when you need to, and don't race when you don't need to. Junior knows that now.

There's just little things like that that the fans don't always see on the racetrack.

He's grown so much and is a lot smarter. He knows not to use a car up. He's just more experienced. He's not as hotheaded anymore. And he's focused. I see that in his eyes.

There's times when I walk by him, and he's thinking about something, something about the race car or the race, and he doesn't even notice I'm there. He wouldn't have done that when he was in Late Model. But he knows there's not much time to be buddies here.

And all that means he'll have success in Winston Cup. He's ready. There's no doubt. He's still a kid, but he's mature in the right ways – and it's in his blood. He's just a natural. Just as soon as he set foot in that No. 3 car, he set the world on fire, and he didn't have to work at the driving part of it.

Every given week, he can do that. A lot of people could get lucky and finish in the top five in the car he has. But every week? That's how you can tell he's a natural.

Dale has the right formula for Winston Cup success: a strong work ethic, maturity and a natural talent. "He's ready," Green says. "There's no doubt."

Jeff Green raced in twenty Winston Cup events in 1998 before devoting almost all of his attention to the Busch series in 1999. Thanks to a strong stretch run, Green overtook Matt Kenseth and claimed the runner-up spot in the Busch series standings with 4,367 points.

Green, also a member of a strong racing family, credits his closeness with brothers David and Mark for his success. "A lot of people helped us along the way, and we got lucky, and we ended up in Busch and Winston Cup," Jeff says. "But all that close contact definitely helped us.

"We laid information on each other, and it never hurts to have another person's opinion, especially one that won't lie to you."

Junior in 1999

Busch Grand National Circuit

1999

Date	Event	Track	Type	Make	Finish	Start	Laps	Laps Completed	Status	Earnings
2/13/99	NAPA Auto Parts 300	Daytona	SS	Chevrolet	14	16	120	120	Running	$30,200
2/20/99	ALLTEL 200	North Carolina	SS	Chevrolet	35	1	197	126	Accident	$15,285
3/6/99	Sam's Town 300	Las Vegas	SS	Chevrolet	6	13	200	200	Running	$36,400
3/13/99	Yellow Freight 300	Atlanta	SS	Chevrolet	2	15	195	195	Running	$32,700
3/20/99	Diamond Hill Plywood 200	Darlington	SS	Chevrolet	11	5	147	146	Running	$17,035
3/27/99	Coca-Cola 300	Texas	SS	Chevrolet	10	12	163	163	Running	$28,600
4/3/99	BellSouth Mobility 320	Nashville	ST	Chevrolet	9	1	320	320	Running	$19,235
4/10/99	Moore's Snacks 250	Bristol	ST	Chevrolet	2	7	250	250	Running	$27,910
4/24/99	Touchstone Energy 300	Talladega	SS	Chevrolet	6	17	113	113	Running	$27,125
5/1/99	Auto Club 300	California	SS	Chevrolet	3	1	150	150	Running	$53,875
5/8/99	New Hampshire 200	New Hampshire	SS	Chevrolet	34	5	200	193	Accident	$17,740
5/14/99	Hardee's 250	Richmond	ST	Chevrolet	32	4	250	201	Rear End	$15,540
5/23/99	First Union 200	Nazareth	SS	Chevrolet	2	3	168	168	Running	$26,325
5/29/99	CarQuest Auto Parts 300	Lowe's	SS	Chevrolet	2	22	200	200	Running	$45,150

Date	Event	Track	Type	Make	Finish	Start	Laps	Laps Completed	Status	Earnings
6/5/99	MBNA Platinum 200	Dover	SS	Chevrolet	1	15	200	200	Running	$44,725
6/12/99	Textilease Medique 300	South Boston	ST	Chevrolet	1	1	300	300	Running	$36,300
6/27/99	Lysol 200	Watkins Glenn	RC	Chevrolet	1	3	82	82	Running	$37,800
7/4/99	DieHard 250	Milwaukee	SS	Chevrolet	3	15	250	250	Running	$27,750
7/17/99	Myrtle Beach 250	Myrtle Beach	ST	Chevrolet	25	1	250	247	Running	$18,780
7/24/99	NAPA AutoCare 250	Pikes Peak	SS	Chevrolet	36	12	239	250	Accident	$19,350
7/31/99	CarQuest Auto Parts 250	Gateway	SS	Chevrolet	1	18	200	200	Running	$51,775
8/6/99	Kroger 200	Indianapolis Raceway	ST	Chevrolet	5	3	155	155	Running	$19,125
8/21/99	NAPA 200	Michigan	SS	Chevrolet	1	3	100	100	Running	$43,650
8/27/99	Food City 250	Bristol	ST	Chevrolet	3	5	250	250	Running	$25,615
9/4/99	Dura Lube 200	Darlington	SS	Chevrolet	12	14	147	146	Running	$17,005
9/10/99	Autolite Platinum 250	Richmond	ST	Chevrolet	1	20	250	250	Running	$34,450
9/25/99	MBNA Gold 200	Dover	SS	Chevrolet	33	3	176	200	Running	$17,300
10/9/99	All Pro Bumper to Bumper 300	Lowe's	SS	Chevrolet	5	20	200	200	Running	$32,450
10/23/99	K-Mart 200	North Carolina	SS	Chevrolet	13	2	197	196	Running	$17,950
10/31/99	Sam's Town 250	Memphis	ST	Chevrolet	2	8	2500	250	Running	$40,475
11/6/99	Outback Steakhouse 200	Phoenix	SS	Chevrolet	2	5	200	200	Running	$41,075
11/13/99	Hotwheels.com 300	Homestead-Miami	SS	Chevrolet	2	8	200	200	Running	$68,700

Starts	Poles	Wins	Top 5s	Top 10s	DNFs	Laps Raced	Total Earned
32	5	6	18	22	4	5,581	$985,845

Winston Cup

1999

Date	Event	Track	Type	Make	Finish	Start	Laps	Laps Completed	Status	Earnings
5/30/99	Coca-Cola 600	Lowe's	SS	Chevrolet	16	8	400	397	Running	$36,250
7/11/99	Jiffy Lube 300	New Hampshire	SS	Chevrolet	43	13	300	44	Ignition	$36,475
8/22/99	Pepsi 400	Michigan	SS	Chevrolet	24	17	200	199	Running	$21,765
9/11/99	Exide Batteries 400	Richmond	ST	Chevrolet	10	21	400	399	Running	$29,905
11/21/99	NAPA 500	Atlanta	SS	Chevrolet	14	13	325	324	Running	$37,700

Starts	Poles	Wins	Top 5s	Top 10s	DNFs	Laps Raced	Total Earned
5	0	0	0	1	1	1,363	$162,095

moving
on up

BY STEVE PARK
As Told to Mike Hembree

"This is not an amateur division. It's a division where you've had to prove yourself to get into it and you still have to prove yourself once you get here."
— Steve Park

The biggest difference in moving from Busch Grand National to Winston Cup is the level of the competition. The horsepower of the engines is different, and the weight of the cars is different, but the competition difference is the big thing. Week in and week out, you're battling guys like Mark Martin and Dale Earnhardt and all the other guys that have been doing this for twenty years.

It can be intimidating at first. Your rookie year is intimidating because you're trying to go out there and do a good job for your team. You're trying to learn, and you're trying to not make mistakes.

Think about being in your first race, and you're Dale Earnhardt Jr., and you're running in the top ten. You mess up and you cause a

"Having the sponsor they have in Budweiser, he's already seeing the tremendous size of the commitment he has to make to fulfill the obligations to the sponsor," Park says.

fifteen-car pileup involving Mark Martin and Dale Jarrett and all the guys who are fighting for a points championship.

That was one of my biggest fears. I wanted to be competitive and to learn, but I also wanted to not mess up too much. You have to try to get the respect of these guys that you'll be racing with year in and year out.

Getting used to the difference in the cars really wasn't that big. You just can't drive a Winston Cup car like a Busch car. You can't drive it like an open-wheel car. You drive it for what it is.

The majority of the time, the main difference between the two type cars is in getting the car to handle with the added weight. With the Busch car, you really need to carry a lot of momentum through the corners because the cars are lighter and down on horse-power. In the Cup car, you seem to have to slow down for the corner, and you have the horsepower

Dale learned the nuances of driving a Winston Cup car by competing in five Winston Cup events in 1999. But teammate Steve Park says that's just the beginning: "It's easier to adapt to the changes in cars than it is adapting to the idea of beating Dale Jarrett week in and week out."

Sponsorship commitments, which can be overwhelming, will keep Dale from having the same kind of hands-on relationship with his crew he enjoyed during much of his Busch run.

Autolite **Spark Plugs**

Dale Jr. relishes
the opportunity
to race dad on
a weekly basis.

Turning over more control of his Winston Cup ride should be easier knowing teammate Park (center) and crew chief Tony Eury Sr. (right) will provide support.

to make that time up on the straightaways.

It's a little bit of a different driving style that you need to make adaptations for.

I made adaptations when I moved from open-wheel cars to Busch cars. If you're a race car driver, it's in your blood, and you learn to adapt. It's easier to adapt to the changes in the cars than it is trying to adapt to the idea of beating Dale Jarrett every week.

Moving from Modified racing to Busch racing was a huge deal at first, but I ran some Craftsman Truck races and some Busch North races, and that kind of helped my learning curve before I came down south to run for Dale. It was a tremendous jump at that time from the open-wheel cars to the fendered cars. But I thought it was a smaller jump from the Busch cars to the Winston Cup cars, except for the competition change.

I really think in Dale Junior's instance it's going to be a little easier than normal. The plan at Dale Earnhardt Inc. is to have an already

Park says one of the main differences between driving a Busch car and a Winston Cup car is weight and horsepower, both crucial in cornering. "With the Busch car, you really need to carry a lot of momentum through the corners because the cars are lighter and down on horsepower," he says. "In the Cup car, you seem to have to get slowed down for the corner, and you have the horsepower to make that time up on the straightaways."

Junior proved he could run with the best in his Winston Cup debut at Charlotte, starting eighth and finishing sixteenth. In the final two of his five Cup races in 1999, Dale placed tenth and fourteenth, respectively.

established team in Winston Cup and then to add a second one (Dale Junior's).

Our team started out with nothing, and we developed it into a Cup team, and now we're sort of duplicating that with Junior's team. We already have the shop, the motors, the research and development, and we're hoping it's going to make his transition a little easier than mine was.

I came out of Busch with just one year there, and he's going to have two. He'll also have the benefit of working with the same team he's worked with the last few years.

We had to start with all new people. We're hoping that's going to make our second team a team that's not going to have to go through some of the growing pains we had.

The thing about driving in Winston Cup is that everything has to be the best. You need to have the best engines, the best equipment and the best people. You need to have it all working, and you need to drive the car hard.

We lacked in all those areas up until about the halfway point this year. I lost much of my first year because of the injuries, so we were behind on things. But we started from scratch.

Now we're at the point where we've got plenty of cars and plenty of good motors and real good horsepower. We've gone through all the steps, and all the areas have gotten better. I'm driving better. The team's jelling better. We're starting to come into our own.

I've only been doing this about a year and a half, but you find out quickly that the only way you learn is by getting out there and racing with these guys. There are guys you can race with the cars touching, and there are guys you need to give plenty of room. And that's all a part of experience.

Running with these guys, you get to know their different styles — who you can run real close with and who you need to be a little careful with. I feel I'm pretty comfortable with everybody out there now, and I've gotten used to all their driving

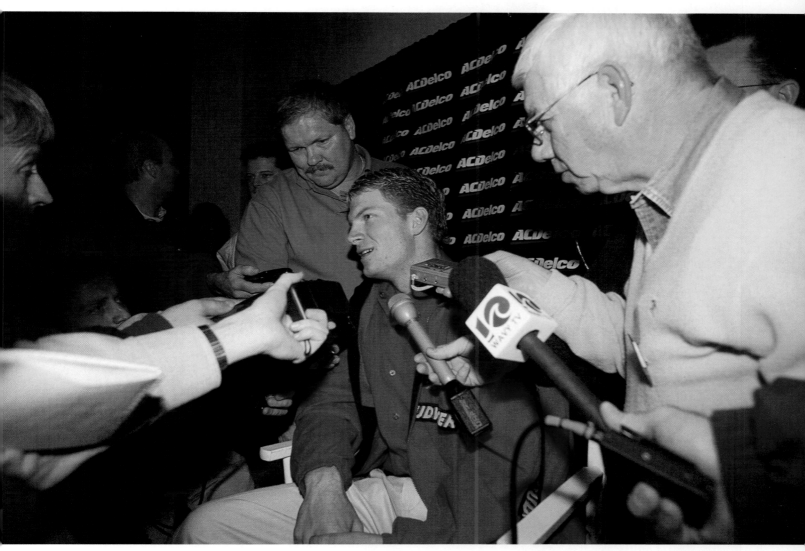

styles. It feels like they've gotten used to mine, too.

Before, a lot of times the veterans would kind of tiptoe around me so that they wouldn't get in trouble. Now I find them having the confidence in me to race side by side and to draft with me and give me a break. You give them a break, and they'll give you a break.

It seems like it took a while to earn that respect, but once you do

get it you get it from almost everybody. This is a very mature division. These guys are true, true professionals. You need to step up to their level and be professional, too, and not do amateur things.

This is not an amateur division. It's a division where you've had to prove yourself to get into it and then you still have to prove yourself once you get here.

You have to have a different

Junior's candor and self-deprecating humor already have made him a favorite among members of the media.

frame of mind in this series. The amount of pressure put on you by the media and the sponsors and stuff more or less triples. Even getting to the race track is tough because there are so many people.

That's another thing you have to adapt to, and it makes your job harder. You have to try to learn the Winston Cup cars and get the experience you need and also fulfill all the added commitments that come along with the additional sponsors and media and everything else that goes along with it.

That part of it stunned me at first, because I grew up building cars and working on them. When I drove for Dale in the Busch series I worked in the shop and helped build the cars and worked side by side with the guys.

The Dale Earnhardt, Inc. team (from left): Steve Park, Dale Earnhardt Sr., Dale Earnhardt Jr. and Ron Hornaday.

Then you go to Cup and you just can't do that. You're not home enough to be able to work side by side with the team, so you need a good leader. You need good people, and you've got to surround yourself with people you can trust. When you step in that race car, you have to be confident you're not getting in a car that's going to fall apart.

A huge part of this is letting go and trusting other people to do the job right. You have to be confident that you can show up at the racetrack on Friday and be able to drive 185 miles per hour and have the car be right.

You move from being a guy who works on his cars to being one who can't be hands-on. You have to put your trust in your team.

I really haven't had to give Dale Jr. much advice. He's been learning on his own. Running the five Winston Cup races in 1999 has given him a taste of what Winston Cup is about.

Having the sponsor he has in Budweiser, he's already seeing the tremendous size of the commitment he has to make to fulfill the obligations to the sponsor. He's getting a wide-open taste of it right now.

Steve Park drives the No. 1 Winston Cup Chevrolets for Dale Earnhardt Inc. and team owner Dale Earnhardt.

A success in NASCAR Modified racing, Park was named to drive for Earnhardt's Busch Grand National team in 1997. He won three races, finished third in the point standings and was named rookie of the year. In 1998, Park moved up to Winston Cup racing in DEI Chevrolets and has shown steady improvement despite a serious accident that sidelined him for half of his first season.

Now his goals include helping Dale Jr. make an even smoother transition.

"We're here not only to help him but also to make this whole team one that can communicate," Park says. "We want to build this into a two-car team that can contend every week in Winston Cup racing."

whiz kid

BY MARK MARTIN
As Told To Monte Dutton

"**I think one thing you notice right away about Dale Jr. is his versatility. He has already . . . won on just about every kind of track.**"
— **Mark Martin**

When people talk to me about Dale Earnhardt Jr., they often talk about how his father brought him along slowly, started him out on the short tracks and made him earn his way up through the ranks. I agree with that, but I also see it from a different viewpoint.

I see it as phenomenal that he's done so well, because, from an outsider's point of view, Dale Jr. didn't show that much interest in driving race cars at an early age. He didn't race all that much until he was well in his teen-aged years. His father definitely didn't make it easy for him, but I find it remarkable that he has shown such maturity so quickly.

Even though you show a personal maturity, which he obviously has, that doesn't make you a mature race-car driver. I've raced in

Earnhardt's rapid rise to Winston Cup has shocked many veteran drivers, including Mark Martin.

some awfully close races with Dale Jr., and I've got to admit that he's won his share of them. I'm very impressed with him, and I'm convinced he has a bright future ahead of him.

I think one thing you notice right away about Dale Jr. is his versatility. He has already, just in his second Busch Grand National season, won on just about every kind of track.

I feel the intermediate-size racetracks are the ultimate test of a driver's skill because of the speed. If it takes thirty seconds to get around, and you're worth two percent, then that's a lot more at a thirty-second track than it is at a sixteen-second track.

It's only a few inches a lap on a small track, but it may be a car length or more on a big track. Learning the cars is more difficult at certain racetracks for any given driver.

One catches on at a big track. Another may get the hang of it first at a small track. One may do well on a flat track, and another may find his way around a banked track best. Dale Jr. seems to have become proficient in an awful big hurry at all those types of tracks. He's even won on a road course already.

Dale Jr., ever since he's been in the blue car (the No. 3 AC Delco Chevrolet), has taken in everything very quickly. Just running with him in Busch Grand National events, I could tell he was processing information very efficiently and making good decisions.

Most people, I think, consider race-car driving to be about being aggressive. What it's actually about is controlling that aggressiveness. You have to process all the information and make good, solid decisions in order to close the deal. You can be doing the best in the world, but you can make one wrong move in the heat of battle and you blow the deal instead of close it.

"Dale Jr., ever since he's been in the blue car, has taken in everything very quickly. Just running with him in Busch Grand National events, I could tell he was processing information very efficiently and making good decisions."
— Mark Martin

Junior has shown he can race well on just about any track, from Bristol's short, high-banking oval, to the mid-sized Rockingham (North Carolina Speedway), Charlotte (Lowe's Motor Speedway) and Dover tracks, to the larger Michigan Speedway, to the futuristic California Speedway.

BRISTOL

ROCKINGHAM

CHARLOTTE

DOVER

MICHIGAN

CALIFORNIA

Dale Jr. knows he can learn plenty about the nuances of the sport from quizzing such sage drivers as Dick Trickle.

"I've raced in some awfully close races with Dale Jr., and I've got to admit that he's won his share of them," Martin says. "I'm very impressed with him, and I'm convinced he has a bright future ahead of him."

In that area, too, Dale Earnhardt Jr. belies his age and years of experience.

It really is no mystery why, in this sport, drivers are able to race at an older age than athletes are able to maintain success in other sports. Part of the secret is this maturity, this ability to control your natural aggressiveness and make the right moves time after time and lap after lap.

There's another fact to that, too. Here in NASCAR, there's less discrepancy in car speeds because the rules are so tight. It comes down to knowing what to do and when to do it.

The advantage of sheer youth is fearlessness and skill. Typically, for a long time, the young driver will show flashier than the old one, but not beat him in the end.

In the end it's that guy who's hit

the wall a hundred times and won't take the chance that the younger driver will. The experienced driver will be smarter and put himself in position to win that race much more often.

What, all of a sudden, we are seeing are drivers like Jeff Gordon and Dale Earnhardt Jr. who seem to have this experience, this ability to save cars and make the right moves at the right time, when they get here. Kids are starting out in this profession almost at the point where they learn to walk, and that's very different than the way it was before.

But Dale Jr. did not start racing when he was five years old, and that makes him even all the more remarkable, at least in my opinion. He was a teen-ager before he even started racing cars, so he's got a very short background, at least compared to many of the other young drivers we are seeing come along.

Is he ready for Winston Cup? I'd say, absolutely. I look forward to having him race with us.

Mark Martin is the most respected driver on the Winston Cup circuit.

That fact was driven home at the end of the 1999 season when Martin, still hunting for his first Cup points title, was named the best "on-track" driver in a poll of NASCAR team members by NASCAR Online.

It wasn't even close: Martin garnered forty-three percent of the vote, compared to eighteen percent for Tony Stewart and sixteen percent for Dale Jarrett.

Martin has come within a whisker of his first title many times, including finishing twenty-six points behind Dale Earnhardt Sr. in 1990. And in 1998 Martin conceded to Jeff Gordon despite posting a career-high seven wins, twenty-two top-fives and twenty-six top-tens and hauling in more than $3 million in prize money.

The Batesville, Arkansas native has finished in the top six in the Winston Cup standings every year since 1988.

like father like son

BY BUDDY BAKER
As Told To Tom Gillispie

"To compare Dale Jr. and Dale Earnhardt, you're talking about a spring colt and a derby winner. The spring colt looks good, but he's still got to get there."
— Buddy Baker

I know something about being the son of a famous driver. At the onset of my career, it came to be a handicap. Hey, I was being compared to one of the best drivers in the world, and second wasn't good enough — third certainly wasn't good enough. It took a while.

In my case, I didn't stay with a family team. I did it the hard way, and I'm glad I did. It taught me the ins and outs of racing, and I wouldn't give that up for anything.

The thing is, what do people expect of you? You're just starting out and you're racing the best drivers in the toughest division in the world. People questioned me. They wondered if I'd make it.

And when I got my first win, they came up to me, patted me on the back and said, "We told you that if you'd hang in there, you'd

The future looks bright for Dale Jr. as the two-time Busch series champion attempts to prove he's ready to race — and win — against the best in NASCAR.

Just because Dale was a Busch Grand National champion doesn't mean he'll become a Winston Cup champion too. But Buddy Baker says Little E has the talent necessary to make the leap.

be a winner. We told you to hang in there, because it's coming." But it's not easy.

With the Earnhardts there are three generations to consider. Ralph Earnhardt, in my opinion, was as good a Late Model driver as there was on a half-mile track. Dale Earnhardt has seven Winston Cup championships and seventy-four wins. That tells you a lot about the man. Dale Earnhardt Jr. shows a lot to me. He looks like an established star, but he's not ready for that yet.

A lot of drivers have won Busch Grand National championships and done nothing in Winston Cup. There are Winston Cup drivers who have struggled, then jumped back down to Busch Grand National and were great. So we'll have to wait and see.

It isn't cut-and-dried because of the ability Dale Jr. showed in Busch Grand National. You have to remember that his father didn't start out with great equipment or an established team that had been

Buddy Baker faced tremendous pressure trying to live up to the standards set by father Buck. "People questioned me," Buddy says. "They wondered if I'd make it."

So much for paying your dues. Richard Petty cut his teeth on the Winston Cup circuit, going on to win a series-record two hundred times. That's a lot of victory cigars.

around a while. He had to develop into a situation.

Most of us have to work our way into the sport like Cale Yarborough, Dale Earnhardt, Mark Martin, myself, the Allisons. We didn't have good equipment to start out with.

Before Dale Earnhardt Jr., the one driver who started out with really good equipment was Richard Petty. Richard walked into the family operation, and he didn't have to go through the various short tracks around the country, the way most of us did. Richard was lucky, but he made the most of it.

The one thing you can say about Dale Earnhardt, though: He sent his kid out in not necessarily the best Late Model equipment and let him hammer around the country. Richard started out in Winston Cup, and he made the most of it.

Richard's probably the quickest study of anybody I've ever seen. After one year, he was racing with the best in the world.

Dale Jr., like Richard, started out last year with an established team. He had help from Steve Park, who drives Winston Cup cars for Dale Sr., as well as crew chief Tony Eury Sr. and Tony Eury Jr. And he has had help from Dale Earnhardt.

I'll say this: Both drivers, Earnhardt and Earnhardt Jr., are very aggressive. When Earnhardt was younger, he was as impatient as Earnhardt Jr. Tony Stewart, who was a great Winston Cup rookie in 1999, was the same. Sometimes he'd show maturity; other times he'd be aggressive.

To compare Dale Jr. and Dale Earnhardt, you're talking about a spring colt and a derby winner. The spring colt looks good, but he's still

With Tony Eury Sr. leading a respected crew, Dale Jr. should be able to focus his full attention on driving during the 2000 season.

Dale Sr.'s luck began to change when he was offered a full-time ride by California businessman and car owner Rod Osterlund for the 1979 Winston Cup season. Earnhardt claimed rookie of the year honors.

got to get there. You can look at a race-car driver, and it's easy to say he's every bit as good as his dad, but it's a totally different deal.

My father, for instance, was always in the national hunt for the championship, and I raced with him a couple of months. He gave me good advice. He said for me to go out and learn on my own, and I was not always in the best equipment.

Dale Earnhardt wasn't very good the first time I raced against him. Frankly, he didn't do enough to warrant anybody's attention. Until he drove the No. 2 car for Rod Osterlund, we didn't pay much attention to him.

I remember him turning over in Will Cronkite's car. You don't jump out there and go, you have to earn

your wings. But when he got the opportunity in Osterlund's car, I thought, "Good Lord!"

He may have been good before that, but he didn't have the opportunity. When he got in a good car, well, the rest is history. I remember saying in Atlanta, "If that guy makes it, the woods are full of them." That shows what I know.

The first time Dale drove for Rod Osterlund at Charlotte, I saw all the qualities his father, Ralph, had, plus some qualities of his own. He had a tremendous amount of ability, and he was relentless, lap after lap. He'd drive as hard as he could drive. I went, "Whoa! Where did this come from?" I found out. So did we all.

I saw Earnhardt Jr. when he raced Late Model Stock at places like Myrtle Beach. I saw him at Nashville. He didn't always have the best equipment, but he had a lot of moxie, a lot of promise.

Then he got into his father's No. 3 Busch Grand National car, and right away you could see he was something special. He is special. It's

Junior's already huge fan following steadily grew in the months leading up to his Winston Cup debut.

Above: "Dale Jr. has a lot of ability, and I think he'll be the national champion in Winston Cup," Baker says. "But he's young."
Below: Dale Jr. has some huge footsteps to follow: seven Winston Cup championships, seventy-four victories, more than $35 million in earnings . . .

all part of growing up. All drivers have to grow up.

The thing is, we're talking about the best drivers in the world. My dad always said that the game's free, but the lessons are expensive, and that's the way I look at it, too.

It's incredible how well the younger drivers develop. Who would have thought Earnhardt Jr. would have been the Busch Grand National champion his first year? He has the ability, but it takes one hundred percent dedication. And it takes a lot away from being a young man.

You can't go out with your buddies or go to the mall when you want to. You have to make sacrifices. You don't want to be pushed to the limit all the time.

Dale Jr. has a lot of ability, and I think he'll be the national champion in Winston Cup. But he's young. I hope he doesn't burn out. That's not fun.

With a young guy like Earnhardt Jr., who has already made a lot of money, he's not concerned about making his next dollar. So I hope the intensity stays where it is. His father knew that racing was his one and only chance at life, I think. It's hard to get that type of dedication. You have to set goals. Dale's father said all he wanted to be was a racer, and I hope Dale Jr. has that burning desire, too.

Me, I wanted to win; I didn't care if it took five months or twenty years. I was in it for the long haul. I won my first major race at twenty-six, so it takes dedication. When things go bad, you can't say, "I'm going to drop out."

You look at Dale Jr. and wonder.

His daddy's won just about everything and been the national champion seven times over. I believe that if he'll stick with it he'll be a champion, too.

Perhaps no person is better situated than Buddy Baker to evaluate Dale Jr.'s talent. In addition to also being the son of a successful NASCAR driver, Buddy teaches at the stock car driving school his father, Buck, started at North Carolina Motor Speedway.

And when Buddy isn't teaching he serves as a television commentator, offering insight into every driver on the Winston Cup circuit.

Baker, like his father, is a member of NASCAR's Hall of Fame, and in 1970 he became the first driver to turn a lap at faster than two hundred miles per hour.

Career Stats

Year	Starts	Wins	2nd	3rd	4th	5th	6–10th	11–37th	DNFs	Poles	Outside Poles	Total Laps	Earnings
1996	1	0	0	0	0	0	0	1	0	0	0	249	$1,880
1997	8	0	0	0	0	0	1	4	4	0	1	1,038	$52,880
1998	31	7	5	2	0	2	6	8	3	3	3	6,000	$1,332,701
1999	32	6	7	3	0	2	4	11	4	5	1	5,581	$985,845
Totals	**72**	**13**	**12**	**5**	**0**	**4**	**11**	**24**	**11**	**8**	**5**	**12,868**	**$2,373,306**

13 Wins

Date	Event	Track	Type	Make	Finish	Start	Laps	Laps Completed	Status	Earnings
4/4/98	Coca-Cola 300	Texas	SS	Chevrolet	1	16	200	200	Running	$66,075
5/30/98	MBNA Platinum 200	Dover	SS	Chevrolet	1	16	200	200	Running	$34,075
7/5/98	DieHard 250	Milwaukee	SS	Chevrolet	1	2	250	250	Running	$39,625
7/5/98	DieHard 250	Milwaukee	SS	Chevrolet	1	2	250	250	Running	$39,625
7/19/98	Kenwood Home & Car Audio 300	California	SS	Chevrolet	1	2	150	150	Running	$68,175
7/31/98	Kroger 200	Indy Raceway Park	ST	Chevrolet	1	16	200	200	Running	$34,225
9/11/98	Autolite Platinum 250	Richmond	SS	Chevrolet	1	2	250	250	Running	$35,600
10/17/98	CarQuest Auto Parts 250	Gateway	SS	Chevrolet	1	13	200	200	Running	$48,525
6/5/99	MBNA Platinum 200	Dover	SS	Chevrolet	1	15	200	200	Running	$44,725
6/12/99	Textilease Medique 300	South Boston	ST	Chevrolet	1	1	300	300	Running	$36,300
6/27/99	Lysol 200	Watkins Glenn	RC	Chevrolet	1	3	82	82	Running	$37,800
7/31/99	CarQuest Auto Parts 250	Gateway	SS	Chevrolet	1	18	200	200	Running	$51,775
8/21/99	NAPA 200	Michigan	SS	Chevrolet	1	3	100	100	Running	$43,650
9/10/99	Autolite Platinum 250	Richmond	ST	Chevrolet	1	20	250	250	Running	$34,450

8 Poles

Date	Event	Track	Type	Make	Finish	Start	Laps	Laps Completed	Status	Earnings
5/17/98	First Union 200	Nazareth	SS	Chevrolet	28	1	188	200	Running	$12,925
3/28/98	Moore's Snacks 250	Bristol	ST	Chevrolet	2	1	250	250	Running	$21,260
7/25/98	Lycos.com 300	South Boston	ST	Chevrolet	13	1	300	299	Running	$16,925
2/20/99	ALLTEL 200	North Carolina	SS	Chevrolet	35	1	197	126	Accident	$15,285
4/3/99	BellSouth Mobility 320	Nashville	ST	Chevrolet	9	1	320	320	Running	$19,235
5/1/99	Auto Club 300	California	SS	Chevrolet	3	1	150	150	Running	$53,875
6/12/99	Textilease Medique 300	South Boston	ST	Chevrolet	1	1	300	300	Running	$36,300
7/17/99	Myrtle Beach 250	Myrtle Beach	ST	Chevrolet	25	1	250	247	Running	$18,780

Firsts and Lasts

First Start: 6/22/96   Myrtle Beach
First Pole: 3/28/98   Bristol Start
First Win: 4/4/98   Texas Start
Last Start: 11/13/99   Miami
Last Pole: 7/17/99   Myrtle Beach
Last Win: 9/10/99   Richmond

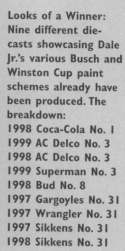

Looks of a Winner: Nine different die-casts showcasing Dale Jr.'s various Busch and Winston Cup paint schemes already have been produced. The breakdown:
1998 Coca-Cola No. 1
1999 AC Delco No. 3
1998 AC Delco No. 3
1999 Superman No. 3
1998 Bud No. 8
1997 Gargoyles No. 31
1997 Wrangler No. 31
1997 Sikkens No. 31
1998 Sikkens No. 31

LOOK FOR THESE OTHER QUALITY RACING BOOKS FROM BECKETT PUBLICATIONS.

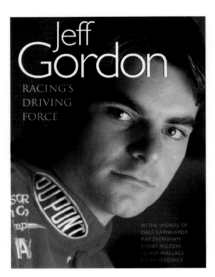

Jeff Gordon:
Racing's Driving Force

The once upstart "kid" is now a 3-time champion and at the pinnacle of his racing career. Many chapters in this photo-intensive book are told in the words of Gordon's racing colleagues or contemporaries. Personalities such as Ray Evernham, Dale Earnhardt, Kenny Wallace and others talk about Gordon's winning spirit, competitiveness and legacy.

128 pages   **$24.95**   **ISBN: 1-887432-85-X**

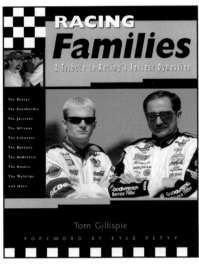

Racing Families:
A Tribute to Racing's Fastest Dynasties

NASCAR can certainly be considered a family tradition. The more than 50-year-old sport has been forged with strong family ties. And many racing family trees contain branches with three generations of drivers. In words and pictures, this book tells the story of the Pettys, the Allisons, the Jarretts, the Labontes, the Earnhardts and nine other families that are the lifeblood of NASCAR.

128 pages   **$24.95**   **ISBN: 1-887432-87-6**

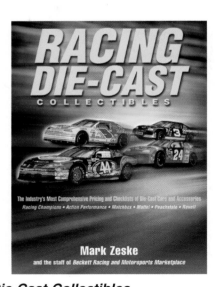

Racing Die-Cast Collectibles

This incredible book features page after page of color photos, pricing and checklists for all scales of racing die-cast cars. Manufacturers listed include Racing Champions, Action Performance, Revell, Winner's Circle, Hot Wheels and many more. Includes sections on how to start your collection and hints for storage and display, plus checklists for the top 12 NASCAR drivers.

256 pages   **$24.95**   **ISBN: 1-887432-81-7**

Beckett Racing Collectibles
and Die-Cast Price Guide No. 5

New edition! Now with the most comprehensive coverage of die-cast cars available anywhere. Includes up-to-date die-cast pricing, plus prices and alphabetical driver listings for every racing card ever issued. Covers NASCAR, IndyCar, Formula One, NHRA, Sprint Cars and more. Over 1,000 card set listings and 6,000 die-cast replica listings.

496 pages   **$14.95**   **ISBN:1-887432-91-4**